Bartering

By Linda Crotta Brennan

Illustrated by Rowan Barnes-Murphy

The Child's World®

Published by The Child's World®
1980 Lookout Drive • Mankato, MN 56003-1705
800-599-READ • www.childsworld.com

Acknowledgments
The Child's World®: Mary Berendes, Publishing Director
The Design Lab: Design and production
Red Line Editorial: Editorial direction

Design elements: Eric Krouse/Dreamstime

ISBN 9781614732402
LCCN 2012932817

Printed in the United States of America
Mankato, MN
July 2012
PA02122

About the Author

Linda Crotta Brennan has a master's degree in early childhood education. She has taught elementary school and worked in a library. Now, she is a full-time writer. She enjoys learning new things and writing about them. She lives with her husband and goofy golden retriever in Rhode Island. She has three grown daughters.

About the Illustrator

Rowan Barnes-Murphy has created images and characters for children's and adults' books. His drawings have appeared in magazines and newspapers all over the world. He's even drawn for greeting cards and board games. He lives and works in Dorset, in southwest England, and spends time in rural France, where he works in an ancient farmhouse.

Tomás leaned across the table where he was sitting. "Hey, Jack, I'll trade you my bean burrito for your peanut butter and jelly sandwich."

Jack shook his head. "No, thanks. I don't like refried beans. I'd rather have Mia's macaroni and cheese."

Mia grinned. "I don't really want peanut butter and jelly. But I will take a bean burrito. Let's do a three-way trade."

"Bartering is something people did a long time ago, right?" asked Tomás.

"Yes, before money was invented, everyone had to barter," said Miss Singh.

"How long ago was that?" asked Jack.

"Well, the first metal coins were invented almost 3,000 years ago," said Miss Singh. "But it took a very long time for money to be commonplace—hundreds and hundreds of years. Even then, people would barter sometimes. For example, they bartered when they met people who didn't use money."

"Like the explorers," said Tomás, "or the settlers. They traded things like tools and guns with Native Americans for fur."

"That's right," Miss Singh replied.

"Why did people invent money?" asked Jack. "Wasn't it easier just to trade stuff? They'd been doing it for a long time already."

"Bartering doesn't always work well," said Miss Singh. "Let's say you need shoes and you have wheat to trade. But the shoemaker already has lots of wheat. He wants something else, perhaps apples or potatoes."

"You could do a three-way trade, like we did," said Jack.

"You could, but you have to find someone with apples who wants wheat. That could take a lot of time," said Miss Singh. "And what if you had big things to trade, such as tables?"

"You'd have to carry your tables around to trade them," said Tomás. "That would be hard work. It would be tiring."

"I could do it!" said Jack, flexing his arms and showing his muscles.

Mia laughed. "If you want to trade apples for a table, the apples might spoil before you found someone with a table."

"That's right," said Miss Singh. "If goods you trade spoil, you'll be in trouble."

"It's easier to carry money than a table or apples," said Tomás. "And you can buy all sorts of things with money. Plus, you don't have to find someone who wants the thing you have to trade."

"Exactly," said Miss Singh.

"So, now we use money instead of bartering, right?" asked Jack.

"We usually use money," explained Miss Singh, "but we still barter. For example, people barter in countries where there isn't much money. They don't have money to spend, so they barter."

"People barter here, too," said Tomás. "After my Uncle Tito retired, he didn't have much money. My mom let him stay in our basement apartment in exchange for watching my brother and me while she's at work."

Is there anything you want to barter? Ideas for things you could trade include things you don't use anymore, something you make, chores you enjoy, and special skills you could share.

"Some people barter online," said Miss Singh. "The Internet has made it easier to find trading **matches**."

"I think my dad did something like that. He found someone online who traded a new desk for my grandfather's antique saw," said Mia.

"Kids trade, too," said Jack. "I traded three of my Red Sox baseball cards for a Reggie Jackson card."

"But you need to be careful when you trade," said Mia. "My friend Reagan traded her extra baseball glove for a soccer ball. And when she got it home, she found out the ball had a hole. She was upset."

"I know how she felt," said Tomás. "My brother said he would take out the trash for me if I gave him my Mets cap. I thought he was going to take out the trash for a whole week, but he only did it once. And he wouldn't give back my cap."

"The best trade is when everyone is happy," said Miss Singh.

"My cousin Hugo and I have a good trade," said Tomás. "I help him clean his room and he helps me clean mine. The job is easier and faster working together. Besides, cleaning together is fun."

"Bartering can help the environment, too," said Mia. "My dad drives his friend to work one week. The next week, the friend drives him. Carpooling saves energy."

"It saves your dad money, too," said Tomás.

"Businesses barter, too," said Mia. "Sam's Ice Cream gives my sister's softball team uniforms and equipment. In exchange, the shop **advertises** its name on the players' jerseys."

"You're right, Mia," Miss Singh responded. "Bartering can be good for business."

"I wonder if our lemonade stand could do a trade," said Mia.

"I'm a really good artist," said Jack. "I'll make signs to advertise your business if you'll give me free lemonade as payment."

"How about if you get one week of free lemonade for each sign you make for us?" asked Tomás.

"That sounds fair to me," said Jack.

Mia and Tomás looked at each other and nodded in agreement.

"Done!" said Tomás.

They did a three-way shake.

Mia grinned. "Another brilliant barter!"

Glossary

advertise (AD-vur-tize): To advertise is to share information about a product or service in order to sell it. Sam's Ice Cream advertises on softball players' jerseys.

barter (BAHR-tur): To swap goods or services without using money is to barter. Tomás bartered lemonade for a sign made by Jack.

goods (gudz): Goods are things to trade or sell. The goods sold at Mia and Tomás's lemonade stand are lemonade and cookies.

match (mach): Two people who agree to a trade are a match. Tomás found a match who was willing to trade a baseball mitt for his hockey stick.

service (SUR-vis): Service is work done for money or a trade. When Tomás bartered lemonade for signs from Jack, he traded his product for Jack's service.

triangular barter (trye-ANG-gyuh-lur BAHR-tur): This is a three-way trade. Mia, Jack, and Tomás swapped lunches in a triangular barter.

Books

Haskins, Lori. *No Money? No Problem!*
New York: Kane, 2004.

Stanley, Sanna. *Monkey for Sale.*
New York: Frances Foster, 2002.

Web Sites

Visit our Web site for links about bartering:
childsworld.com/links

Note to Parents, Teachers, and Librarians:
We routinely verify our Web links to make sure
they are safe and active sites. So encourage
your readers to check them out!

Index